An illustrated souvenir

THE NATIONAL TRUST ESTATE ON

HADRIAN'S WALL

FROM HOUSESTEADS TO CAWFIELDS

Northumberland

The National Trust

Introduction

In the year AD 122, the Emperor Hadrian, alarmed by the inability of the loose-knit defences of the occupying Roman army to control the tribes in the North of England, ordered the construction of a defensive barrier from the Tyne to the Solway Firth.

The National Trust's six-mile stretch of this Wall, from Housesteads to Cawfields in the central sector, includes one of the thirteen forts and five of the eighty milecastles which punctuate its full length. Although a small proportion, it is a significant one, for elsewhere much of the original Wall is no longer apparent. Some of its stones lie beneath the streets of Newcastle or the east–west Military Road constructed in the 18th century, and some can be identified in the walls of local farm buildings.

Visitors to this stretch will be rewarded by views of the remains of military works which many centuries ago constituted the northern frontier of the Roman Empire, set in landscape of incomparable grandeur.

Peel Crags

The Wall at the Knag Burn. The Burn runs under the Wall beneath culverts between the gateway and the fort at Housesteads

Crag Lough, looking westwards from Hotbank. On Whinshield in the distance the Wall reaches its highest point

Housesteads Fort – the Setting

National Trust Information Centre, rebuilt after destruction by fire in June 1984

The fort of Housesteads (the English name generally preferred to various Roman versions of which Vercovicius is the most common) lies half a mile to the north of the National Trust Information Centre on the Newcastle upon Tyne – Chollerford – Greenhead – Carlisle road. The visitor comes first to some remains of the 'vicus' or civilian settlement which once catered for the off-duty hours of the garrison; they nestle below the robust stone of the fort walls. To the west are Housesteads farmhouse and the museum (a scaled reconstruction of a vicus building) which contains models of the fort and of Hadrian's Wall, and some of the fruits of excavation in the area. The fort hugs the contours of a dolerite ridge, the ground sloping upwards from the south and levelling out as it approaches the north rampart, which laps the very edge of the steep drop to the rushy field below. It dominates the approach from the north through the gentle Knag Burn defile, with natural protection provided on either side by steep ridge faces.

Around the fort a landscape unfolds of great bare grassland fields confined by walls and studded by modest stone farm buildings and occasional woods and shelter-belts of windswept trees, whose roots cling to the shallow soil clothing the limestone rock. The huge Northumbrian skies emphasise the drama of the scene. It may not, however, have been the view which met the eyes of the soldiers who occupied the fort for two centuries or more; in those days the rolling countryside was probably covered with thorn and scrub, which made way centuries later for turf clipped by sheep, while the monotonous blocks of coniferous woodland lying to the north are 20th-century innovations – part of the largest man-made forest in the United Kingdom.

Model of the fort, showing the civilian settlement to its south, in the Housesteads Museum

Aerial view of Housesteads from the south, with the farm buildings and museum to its south-west, the Wall running north-east over the Knag Burn and westwards through Housesteads Wood. Broomlee Lough lies to its north, and traces of the civilian settlement can be seen south of the fort

The Layout of the Fort

The permanent forts of the Roman army followed a regulation pattern. It is customary to liken their outline to the rectangular shape and rounded corners of playing-cards. At Housesteads, as elsewhere, the ramparts were pierced on each side by a gateway of dressed stone, closed by double wooden gates turning in pivot-holes which can still be seen. On either side of these gateways were guardrooms. There were angle-towers at each corner of the fort and other towers at intervals between.

Streets divided the fort area and at a crossroads near the centre stood the headquarters building containing the administrative offices, the great hall used for ceremonial and official occasions, and the regimental shrine in which the unit's standards were kept. Next to it was the commandant's house, of a size befitting the rank and status of a Roman officer and large enough to accommodate his family and his servants. Barrack rooms for the soldiers, granaries and a hospital were standard within the layout. Baths, always a feature of Roman life, were often sited apart from the fort itself. At Housesteads they lay several hundred yards away in the Knag Burn but there is virtually nothing of them to be seen. It is doubtful if they could have been very sophisticated, for water supply must always have been a problem.

Each of the Wall forts has its particular features of interest today; in the case of Housesteads the massive gateways, the granaries and the ingenious and well-preserved latrine system remain especially in the memory.

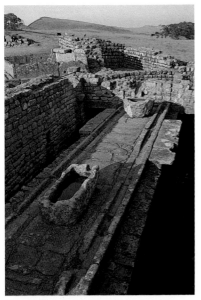

The Latrine, with stone basins in the central part and deep sewers either side, over which seats were placed. Behind is a large water cistern

West Gateway. The robust stone piers supported wooden doors pivoting on holes in the lintel and base

Housesteads, the South Granary. The stone piers supported ventilated wooden flooring for the storage of grain

The Roman Army at Housesteads

The builders of the Wall and of its forts were legionaries, the elite of the Imperial army, recruited exclusively from Roman citizens. They had the technical knowledge, skills and experience to plan and construct this frontier barrier but it was not their task to garrison it. When the work was completed they returned to their bases in York, Chester or Caerleon and to their role as a highly professional, heavy infantry reserve. The manning of the completed defences was left to auxiliaries, whose officers came from Rome and soldiers largely from Germany and the Low Countries.

These auxiliaries served for up to twenty-five years and were rewarded at the end of their service with Roman citizenship, which applied also to their children. They were equipped with a woollen cloak worn over leather tunic and trousers, a helmet of iron or bronze, a mail shirt and a flat, oval leather-covered shield. Arms consisted of a spear or sword and a dagger. Cavalry rode without stirrups. Food and housing were certainly adequate, and the vicus (civilian settlement) outside the fort walls included shops, inns and accommodation of sorts for garrison families.

Auxiliary infantryman, 2nd century AD. Life-size model in the museum

A barrack in the north-east corner of the fort, divided into living quarters, each for eight men

The Knag Burn approach to the rounded north-east corner of Housesteads Fort

The Construction of the Wall

Junction of wall construction by different gangs

Hadrian's original conception was for a continuous wall from east to west with milecastles every Roman mile (1620 yards) and turrets in between, every third of a mile. The Wall's outer faces were constructed of dressed stones of rectangular shape, wedged and fixed in mortar, with a core of rubble bonded with mortar or puddled clay. Where suitable local stone was not available (in the western section) turf walls were built at first. Originally the breadth of the Wall was ten feet and the height about fifteen feet, probably with a parapet to the north. The breadth was later reduced to eight feet.

It was not envisaged that there would be forts in the actual line of the Wall; the reserve forces would be stationed in depth in forts to the south, such as Chesterholme. However, the policy changed and thirteen were built forward in the front line. If the topography allowed, they were constructed athwart the Wall; elsewhere, as at Housesteads, the Wall itself was their northern rampart.

Horizontal coursing on a steep slope, west of Crag Lough

The northern rampart of Housesteads Fort, with the Knag Burn Gate in the background. To allow for a broad fighting platform, there was an earth bank behind this rampart in Roman times. It was removed when the fort was excavated in the 19th century

Milecastles and Turrets

The North Gate of Milecastle 37 after
consolidation in 1989

Visitors often find the remains of milecastles unimpressive. Usually there is little to see apart from the outside walls (eight to ten feet broad) surrounding turf-covered rubble and fallen masonry. It requires imagination to visualise the routine life of some thirty-two Roman auxiliaries in this modest enclosure. One half of the interior provided accommodation for the soldiers and the other, storage and cooking facilities. The North Gate, surmounted by a tower, could be used as a sally-port by the auxiliaries if called upon to attack raiding parties. It and the gate in the south wall were originally wide enough to allow the passage and inspection of wagons carrying produce and possessions. Later these gateways were narrowed; examples may be seen at Milecastles 37 and 39.

In the stretch between Housesteads and Steel Rigg, Milecastle 37, a little west of Housesteads, is notable for some fine dressed stone arch sections, some of which have now been replaced in their original position. Milecastle 39 is perhaps remarkable for its apparently vulnerable site in a nick in the ridge – it is even known as Castle Nick. Of Milecastle 38, between them and to the south of Hotbank Farm, little trace remains.

The same applies to the turrets which lay, two between each milecastle, at distances of 540 yards. They were two-storey signalling towers twenty feet square, manned from the garrisons of the milecastles. In due course, as an economy measure, some of the turrets were dismantled and the National Trust estate has little evidence of any of them.

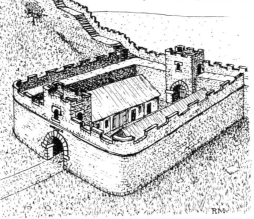

Milecastle 39 in the 2nd century AD – an
artist's impression for comparison with the
photograph opposite

Milecastle 39 after archaeological
excavation and consolidation

The Ditch, the Vallum and the Military Way

The Wall Ditch at Milking Gap

The Wall, Vallum and Military Way, aerial view. The Wall here follows the line of the crags. The well-defined Vallum on the right provided security control from the south. The Military Way, for administrative use, wound between the two. Shield on the Wall Farm in the upper part of the view was acquired by the National Trust in 1987. The land in the foreground, embracing Milecastle 42 (English Heritage), is part of Cawfields Farm acquired by the Trust in 1992

There was more to the Wall than its forts, milecastles and turrets. Immediately to the north, its defences were strengthened by a ditch, continuous except where natural features such as cliffs or water made this unnecessary. The depth of this ditch varied from ten to twenty feet; its breadth thirty to forty feet; and it was sited an average twenty feet or so from the Wall.

To the south, at a distance from the Wall which varies from a few feet to hundreds of yards, ran the Vallum, another ditch but this time without tactical significance. Its depth was ten feet, its breadth at the top twenty, tapering to eight feet at its flat bottom. The spoil from the ditch was piled in low continuous mounds away from the edge. At intervals there were crossing points, probably designed to control civilian access, the Vallum itself forming the southern perimeter of army territory.

The Military Way was an administrative road between Wall and Vallum for the supply of the garrison and it followed the line of least topographical resistance, ignoring tactical considerations. To this day its route can be identified by the difference between its turf surface and the grass fields which it traverses and the fact that field gates are traditionally sited upon it, for the sound Roman foundations of the road still stand the farmer in good stead.

These three man-made features together complemented the basic conception of the frontier wall, giving added defensive strength, security control over approach from the south, and logistical support for the garrison.

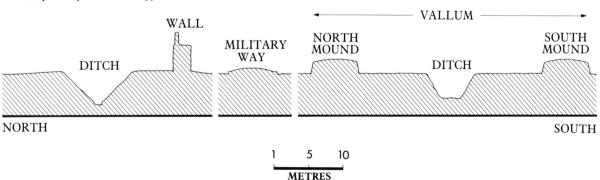

Crag Lough from Steel Rigg, with
Hotbank Farm and the Wall beyond

Housesteads to Rapishaw Gap

One of the most heavily trodden stretches of the Wall runs westwards from the ramparts of the Fort, through the pine trees of Housesteads Wood. It provides for many people their first close view of Hadrian's line of defence against the tribes to the north. The bare earth of its top, once turf-covered, shows the damage wrought by the pressure of visitors. Northwards lies Broomlee Lough, framed by bare fields and forestry; to the south, evidence of cultivation terraces from Roman and later times supplies a foreground to a panorama of south Northumberland and the Durham moors.

The walker soon comes to Milecastle 37, with its sharp land-fall to the north, which surely made impracticable any military threat or commercial transit. Further west, the ground slopes steeply downwards, levels out and climbs again to the unforgettable, unsur-passable eastwards view from Cuddy's Crags, with the Wall winding along the edges of the bluffs and ridges to the distant skyline. Further on still, the land drops to the first of the 'gaps' in this section, Rapishaw Gap, through which the Pennine Way follows the line of an old limestone road, on which, four hundred yards to the south, a fine example of the many early limekilns in this area can be seen.

The Wall-top walk in Housesteads Wood, leading to Milecastle 37

19th-century limekiln near Rapishaw Gap, since restored by the National Trust

Hadrian's Wall, west of Housesteads in 1985. The worn brown areas on the top of the Wall show the serious erosion caused by foot traffic. The path now runs beside the Wall to help preservation

Rapishaw Gap to Milking Gap

National Trust path conservation in Crag Lough Wood. Without such stiles the dry-stone walls would suffer from the many visitors

From Rapishaw a short exacting climb leads to the stretch of Wall which runs along Hotbank Crags. From here in fine weather four loughs can be seen: Broomlee, Greenlee, Crag and Grindon. To the north the density of Kielder Forest embraces the Water Authority's immense new reservoir and beyond this are the Cheviot and Simonside Hills. A mile or so to the south is heather-covered Barcombe Hill which supplied much of the stone for the construction of this section of Wall. More distant, among the woods to the south-east, can sometimes be seen the battlements of Langley Castle and the prominent chimney beyond it.

Six hundred yards to the south and 200 feet below the Wall which is its northern boundary lies Bradley Farm, invisible from here because of the steep slope into the base of which its buildings are tucked. At the end of the crags the Wall turns south-west with the fall of land, revealing the much-photographed glimpse of the roofs of Hotbank seen through pine-trees and beyond it the glinting presence of Crag Lough and on, to the stone curtain of Peel Crags and the distant heights of Winshield. It is surprising that most of the windows of Hotbank Farm face the other way, missing this ravishing vista. The Wall skirts the farm to the east and shortly afterwards passes the remains of Milecastle 38 and a well-defined section of the Ditch before turning westward towards the lough.

Hotbank Farm from the south-west. It nestles into the flank of the hill, with the Wall running laterally behind it and the copse breaking the force of northerly gales

View from Hotbank Farm of Crag Lough and Highshield Crags

Crag Lough

For miles around, Crag Lough dominates the Wall landscape. The surface of its shallow water, reflecting an ephemeral sky pattern, varies from sinister inky blackness to silver to cobalt to verdigris. Its texture can be glassy-still, or whipped by gales or wind-flecked. On its southern bank, almost always in shade, the towering, vertical bluff of the Whin Sill forms a backcloth complementing the mutation of the lake surface. It is not easy to imagine Crag Lough in a military context, for such a setting should surely have made formal defences unnecessary.

Nevertheless, the spectacular heights were once crowned by the regulation Roman cordon of Hadrian's Wall which today is hardly perceptible, for its stones, fallen and turf-covered, have become a bank surmounted by a wire fence. The waters of the lough give hospitality to imperious mute swans and busy coots, mallard, tufted duck and goldeneye; while below the surface trout search for water snails or rise to the fly. Thus Crag Lough gives pleasure to the ornithologist, sport to the fisherman and inspiration to the photographer and the artist. The walker on the heights and the rock climber searching for a hand-hold can, if unafraid of vertigo, look downwards at the miniature world beneath, of tiny waterfowl and toy-like boats, serene upon a mirror setting.

The Lough, seen from the heights of Highshield Crags

Snow scene. Crag Lough from Hotbank

Boats on Crag Lough

Highshield Crags to Peel Crags

The fine stretch of Wall on Peel Crags, restored in 1910

Hard pinnacles of rock rise vertically above scree fragments at the western edge of Crag Lough. The path along the top leads sharply down a slope which required special techniques of the legionary builders of the Wall. Whereas in most sections the stone courses run parallel to the contours of the ground, when the gradient became extreme the courses were stepped horizontally, anchored into the slope. Here they are held together by mortar of a particularly tenacious character.

At the foot of the steep slope a sycamore stands in a position of solitary importance. Beside it, recent excavations have revealed a length of wall seven feet six inches high and fragments of pottery which enable the work to be dated from the late 2nd century; in other words the original Wall must have collapsed or been destroyed, and then rebuilt.

To its west the ground climbs to a knoll which overlooks Milecastle 39, orthodox in measurements but with none of the usual massive gateway masonry – probably because transport difficulties made relatively smaller facing stone more practical. Cat Stairs lead away sharply up to Peel Crags, where a particularly good stretch of Wall, restored in 1910, surmounts dramatic cliffs. Half way along, remains of a demolished turret can be identified by unusually long stones embedded in the replacement Wall. The grassy uplands make easy walking, and easy grazing too for the sheep which are their principal inhabitants.

The view southwards from the Wall at Hotbank Farm

Peel Crags from the north with rock climbers

Peel Crags to Steel Rigg

At the western end of Peel Crags the Wall turns south, following the edge of the re-entrant thought possibly to have skirted an area of marsh in early days. From here the descent from the heights is as steep as anywhere in this section of the Wall. Walkers are well served by the stone steps set in its slope by National Trust wardens. At their foot the Wall loops round to reassert its line and cross the narrow road just below the Steel Rigg car park. Here the National Park authority provides unobtrusive facilities for visitors planning to walk westwards over the heights of Winshield (the Wall's highest point at 1230 feet above sea level) or perhaps to reverse the order of the journey described in previous pages. Those lacking the energy or inclination to tackle the walk in either direction can enjoy a good turf-topped stretch, a hundred and fifty yards to the south of the car park. Few people can fail to sense the high drama of this place, with its vision of Hadrian's frontier defences undulating eastwards through the bare Northumbrian farmland, above Crag Lough and on past Hotbank Farm to Housesteads and beyond.

Steps on Peel Crags constructed by National Trust wardens on a precipitous slope. The technique of stone pitching, a less formal type of path construction appropriate to uplands, has now been introduced on the estate

The north slopes. No ditch in front of the Wall was necessary or practicable here!

Peel Crags from the west in 1984. The Wall in the foreground was excavated in 1986–87 prior to consolidation

Archaeology and Conservation

Although Hadrian's Wall attracted the interest of antiquaries from Elizabethan times, the central sector lay in a lawless border region and it was not until the early 18th century that Housesteads could be easily visited. It quickly established a reputation for its assembled relics. The first true excavation took place in the 1830s and by the middle of the century the Wall on Hotbank Crags and in Peel Gap, the curtain walls of the fort and the milecastles had been uncovered. Excavation in 1898 established the fort's interior plan – one of the first known anywhere in the Roman Empire.

The 20th century has seen much greater activity, including restoration of the fine stretch at Peel Crags in 1910 and excavation of the Housesteads vicus in the 1930s and the fort interior from the 1960s onwards. Previously, local landowners had used estate staff to restore fallen stones and to cap the Wall with turf. This has given way in places to the more thorough and exact techniques of modern archaeology. The National Trust seeks to maintain the Wall in the condition in which it was acquired in 1942. Where necessary, sections are excavated and consolidated with mortar, helped by grant aid from English Heritage. It is the task of the Trust's wardens to conserve the fabric of the Wall, rendering first-aid where the ravages wrought by extremes of weather require it and reinforcing paths and steps to reduce the worst effects of visitor pressure.

National Trust warden repairing damage to the Wall. The drystone sections are vulnerable to the pressure of walkers and to extremes of weather

James Crow, Director of Excavations for the National Trust 1981–8, hard at work

Archaeological excavation in progress, as a prelude to consolidation, at Sycamore Gap in 1983

Farming on the Wall

The National Trust's 1200-hectare (3000-acre) Hadrian's Wall estate runs narrowly either side of the Wall for about six miles, split between five tenanted farms varying in size from 480–90 hectares (1200–220 acres). Farming methods are traditional, for the land offers little scope for innovation, being essentially grazing, unsuitable for arable cultivation. Farms tend to be family-managed, greatly helped by government subsidy, their buildings giving little inside shelter for wintering stock. Life follows the local agricultural cycle: lambing (in these parts a farmer's wife may have to nurse in her kitchen lambs rescued from snow drifts), calving of suckler cows, sheep shearing, fattening for sales and so on. The local agricultural shows are a magnet and these include the annual Roman Wall show, held on the Trust's Hotbank Farm.

Cattle and sheep must be hardy enough to face the harsh climate. Each tenant has his preference but typically the rusty black Galloway, smooth black Aberdeen Angus and blue-grey cross cattle tend to be favoured, and blackface or Swaledale sheep, sometimes crossed with Blue Leicester, produce 'mules' for breeding and fattening. Skilled sheep dogs are essential but shepherding on horse-back has declined in favour of the use of all-terrain vehicles. Thoughtless walkers on the Wall present problems. Farmers understandably react angrily when gates are left open or stock are injured by broken bottles, abandoned empty cans or uncontrolled dogs.

A farmer and his dogs: Thomas Carr (1921–96), a shepherd like his father, was the farmer at Housesteads and Bradley until 1986

Bradley Farm, tucked into the base of the hill. Its roadway crosses a good stretch of Vallum. Hotbank Farm is just over the horizon

Galloway from Hotbank Farm, standing in the shallow waters of Crag Lough